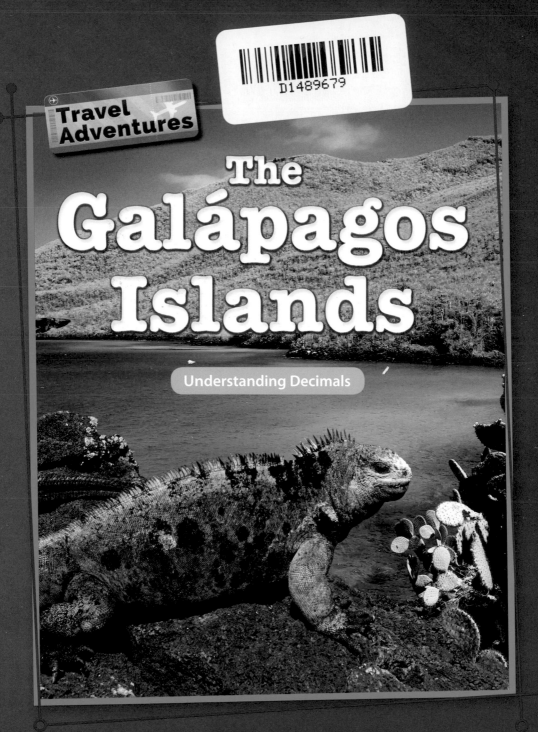

Travel Adventures

The Galápagos Islands

Understanding Decimals

Lauren Altermatt and Dona Herweck Rice

Consultants

Lisa Ellick, M.A.
Math Specialist
Norfolk Public Schools

Pamela Estrada, M.S.Ed.
Teacher
Westminster School District

Publishing Credits

Rachelle Cracchiolo, M.S.Ed., *Publisher*
Conni Medina, M.A.Ed., *Managing Editor*
Dona Herweck Rice, *Series Developer*
Emily R. Smith, M.A.Ed., *Series Developer*
Diana Kenney, M.A.Ed., NBCT, *Content Director*
Stacy Monsman, M.A., *Editor*
Kevin Panter, *Graphic Designer*

Image Credits: P.6 Courtesy of NASA; p.14 Tui De Roy/Minden Pictures/Getty Images; p.16 Mark Moffet/Minden Pictures; p.21 (top) All Canada Photos/Alamy; p.24 (top) Getty Images; p.24 (bottom) Eric Rorer/Aurora Photos/Alamy; p.25 Bernard Bisson/ Getty Images; p.29 Aurora Photos/Alamy; all other images from iStock and/or Shutterstock.

Library of Congress Cataloging-in-Publication Data

Names: Rice, Dona, author. | Altermatt, Lauren, author.
Title: Travel adventures : the Galápagos islands / Dona Herweck Rice and Lauren Altermatt.
Other titles: Galâapagos islands
Description: Huntington Beach, CA : Teacher Created Materials, [2018] | Audience: Grade 4 to 6. | Includes index.
Identifiers: LCCN 2017029057 (print) | LCCN 2017031953 (ebook) | ISBN 9781425859640 (eBook) | ISBN 9781425858186 (pbk.)
Subjects: LCSH: Animals--Galapagos Islands--Juvenile literature. | Galapagos Islands--Juvenile literature.
Classification: LCC F3741.G2 (ebook) | LCC F3741.G2 R48 2018 (print) | DDC 986.6/5--dc23
LC record available at https://lccn.loc.gov/2017029057

Teacher Created Materials

5301 Oceanus Drive
Huntington Beach, CA 92649-1030
http://www.tcmpub.com

ISBN 978-1-4258-5818-6

© 2018 Teacher Created Materials, Inc.

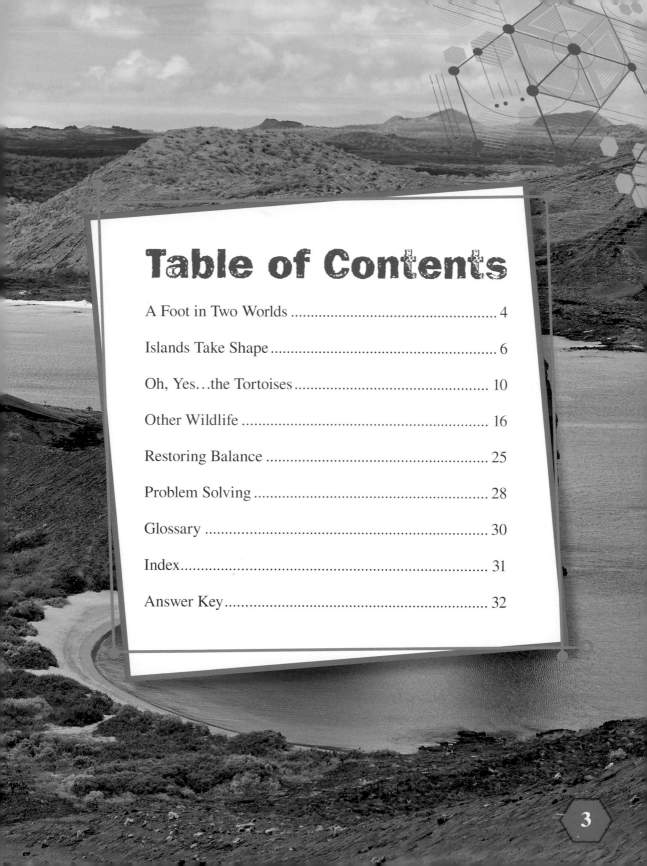

Table of Contents

A Foot in Two Worlds 4

Islands Take Shape 6

Oh, Yes…the Tortoises 10

Other Wildlife 16

Restoring Balance 25

Problem Solving 28

Glossary 30

Index 31

Answer Key 32

A Foot in Two Worlds

Have you ever imagined ruling the world? Standing with a foot on each half of the planet might be a good place to start! If you go to the Galápagos Islands, that's exactly what you can do.

The Galápagos Islands run right through the middle of Earth. This is where the invisible line called the equator lies. Part of the island chain rests in the Northern **Hemisphere**. The other part stretches into the Southern Hemisphere. You can go to the islands and stand with a foot in each half of the planet!

But that's not the only way these islands have a foot in two worlds. They are also part of an old world and a new world. The natural world of the islands is an ancient one. It is rich in color and wildlife. The islands are also part of the modern world of tourism and **resources**. This is a world in which people in fishing and farming **industries** compete to make their livings. They need the resources the islands offer. Striking a healthy balance can be as challenging as bringing two worlds together!

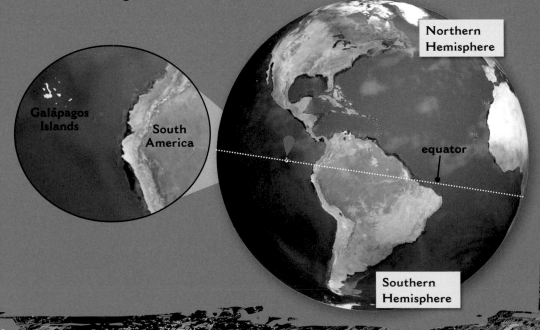

Galápagos Islands

South America

Northern Hemisphere

equator

Southern Hemisphere

LET'S EXPLORE MATH

Sea cucumber fishing is an important industry on the Galápagos Islands. Imagine that the crew of a fishing boat catches 108 sea cucumbers. The crew of a different fishing boat catches 89 sea cucumbers. How is the value of the digit 8 different in each number?

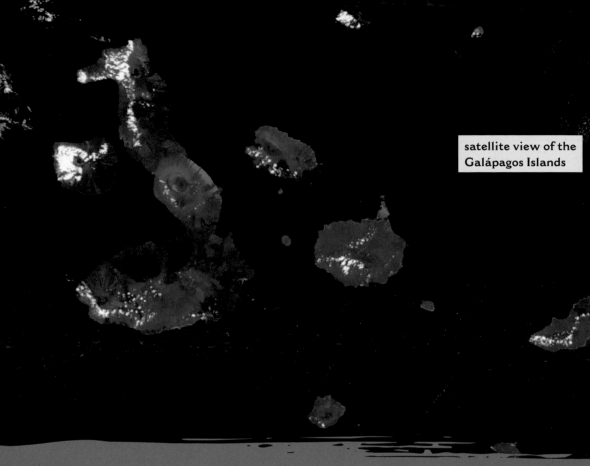

satellite view of the Galápagos Islands

Islands Take Shape

There is no place on Earth like the Galápagos Islands. Made of about 20 main islands, they are like a living museum. Unusual animals thrive. Lush and diverse plants make the **archipelago** (ahr-kuh-PEH-luh-goh) their home. Currents from three oceans meet there. Scientists say this helps to create the variety of sea life that lives on the islands. The islands also mark the spot where three of Earth's **tectonic** plates meet. This helped to create the islands themselves.

The Galápagos Islands are found in the Pacific Ocean. They are strung like beads in the sea, far from the mainland. They are part of Ecuador, which is about 620 miles (1,000 kilometers) away.

Isabela is the largest of the islands. It was named for the queen of Spain. It makes up more than half of the island chain's total landmass. Isabela is still growing. In fact, new islands are always being formed. Older islands move farther and farther away from the hotspot that forms them all. The oldest islands began to take shape millions of years ago. Now, many have vanished below the ocean's surface.

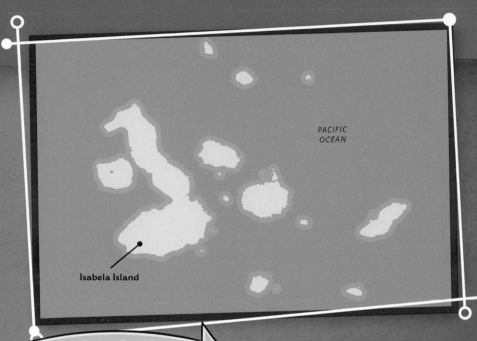

PACIFIC
OCEAN

Isabela Island

LET'S EXPLORE MATH

Isabela makes up about 0.75 of the total landmass of the Galápagos Islands.

1. Color a hundredths grid to show 0.75.

2. In 0.75, what is the value of the digit 7? What is the value of the digit 5? Use the hundredths grid to help you.

Hundredths Grid

Change

The changing shape of the islands is like the changing plant and animal life there—all have evolved over time. Famed scientist Charles Darwin visited the islands in the 1830s. What he saw helped to form his theory of evolution. It had a big effect on how scientists see the growth and change of living things. Darwin said that life **adapts** to its environment. Living things change over time to survive. Adaptations that are most **viable** help things thrive. This idea is also called "survival of the fittest." It means that things most suited to survive will do just that. Things that don't adapt die out over time.

Part of the appeal of the islands is the number of species found there. The climate and resources make the islands an ideal place for them to prosper. Such a wealth of things to see and study remains a big draw for scientists today. In fact, the islands are mainly set aside to be studied and **preserved**. They are some of the most protected lands in all the world.

1. Geospiza magnirostris.
2. Geospiza fortis.
3. Geospiza parvula.
4. Certhidea olivasea.

Charles Darwin

Darwin drew these finches and their beaks in 1889.

Sally Lightfoot crab

sea lion

marine iguana

Oh, Yes...the Tortoises

The first thing that comes to mind when people think about the Galápagos Islands may not be the changing geography. It is probably not the climate. It may not be the scientists there or the islands' history. These are interesting. But one thing seems to interest people more than any other—the tortoises!

Tortoises are a vital part of animal life in the islands. In fact, the island chain is named for them. Spanish sailors discovered the islands about 500 years ago. They saw tortoises everywhere. So, they named the islands with the Spanish word for tortoise and for its shell, or saddle. The word is *galápago*.

giant tortoise

This giant tortoise is about 150 to 200 years old.

By the Numbers

There are about 15,000 tortoises living in the islands today. That is much fewer than once lived there. But they still take up a lot of space! Each one can become huge. They weigh only about 3 ounces (0.09 kilograms) when hatched. But, they can grow to more than 6 feet (1.8 meters) long and weigh 500 pounds (227 kilograms). They also live long. Some are more than 100 years old.

LET'S EXPLORE MATH

A tortoise can grow up to 1.8 meters long.

1. Complete the equations to find the total lengths of 10, 100, and 1,000 tortoises:

   a. $1.8 \times 10 =$

   b. $1.8 \times 100 =$

   c. $1.8 \times 1,000 =$

2. What patterns do you see in your answers? Why do you think this happened?

This tortoise came from a round egg that was about 50 millimeters across.

Adaptations

Galápagos tortoises are herbivores, but not all tortoises are the same. Each of the main islands has a tortoise subspecies that has adapted to the island's conditions. Desert tortoises have few food options available to them. They have adapted to need little food. They must also reach food that grows off the ground. They have developed a unique shell to do so. The shell has a notch at the neck, so the tortoise can stretch its neck to reach food up high.

Giant tortoises move the most in the early morning and late afternoon.

Dangers

Tortoises are reptiles and, therefore, lay eggs. Female tortoises make holes in the ground. They lay their eggs in the holes. They cover the nests to protect their eggs. But, they do not stay with the eggs. In a few months, the eggs hatch. The hatchlings must rely on their instincts to survive. Many do not. Predators, such as hawks, eat many eggs and hatchlings.

Humans are also a danger to tortoises. Humans have brought animals to the islands that prey on tortoises. They have also destroyed island habitats, and hunters **poach**, or illegally hunt, adult tortoises. All these factors reduced the number of tortoises on the islands.

LET'S EXPLORE MATH

Imagine that a tortoise stretches its neck 7.7 centimeters to reach its food. How are the values of each digit different? How are the values of each digit related?

Giant Tortoise Fun Facts

Since the islands became a national park in 1959, tortoises have been protected. People work year-round to restore them to the healthy numbers they once knew.

Many factors make tortoises interesting and fun to study. For example, the gender of hatchlings is influenced by temperature. Eggs that are exposed to low temperatures produce more males. Female tortoises dig for hours when making their nests. They urinate often into the hole to soften the ground. Then, they lay eggs the size of tennis balls.

Once hatched, it takes about a month for hatchlings to dig out of the nests. The first few years of life are filled with dangers for the small tortoises. If they live that long, they have a good chance of growing very old. Tortoises become adults at 20 to 30 years of age.

Hundreds of thousands of tortoises once lived in the islands. On Pinta Island, a single tortoise of its subspecies lived after all the others had died. His name was Lonesome George. He became famous around the world. George died in 2012.

Young tortoises eat the stems of local grasses at a breeding center.

Lonesome George

LET'S EXPLORE MATH

A hatchling weighs about 0.09 kilograms.

1. Draw the number line shown below and label the missing decimals. Then, plot a point to show 0.09.

```
0          0.05          0.10
```

2. Write 0.09 as a fraction.

3. Is 0.09 closer to 0.01 or 0.10? How do you know?

Other Wildlife

People may expect to see a wide range of animals in the Galápagos Islands, but that is not the case. The islands are far from the mainland. New land animals cannot easily reach them. And, the miles of sea in between are not always easy for ocean wildlife to cross. Many animals in the islands were first brought there by humans. Some of them, such as rats and goats, have been destructive to other species. For example, goats killed off the tortoise population on Pinta Island. At first, three goats were placed there. In time, the numbers grew. Herds of goats trampled tortoise nests and habitats.

wild goats

The great blue heron and lava lizard are native to the Galápagos Islands.

Of course, there are animal species in the islands that were there long before humans. If you visit, you may see many of them. Compared to other places in the **tropics**, the range of animal species is low. Other places may be home to thousands of species. But, these islands have little more than 200 known species of mammals, birds, and reptiles.

Since the time that the islands became a national park, the numbers of animals living there has grown. Habitats are protected better than they have been since people found the islands. Care is taken to protect wildlife from invasive species and hunters.

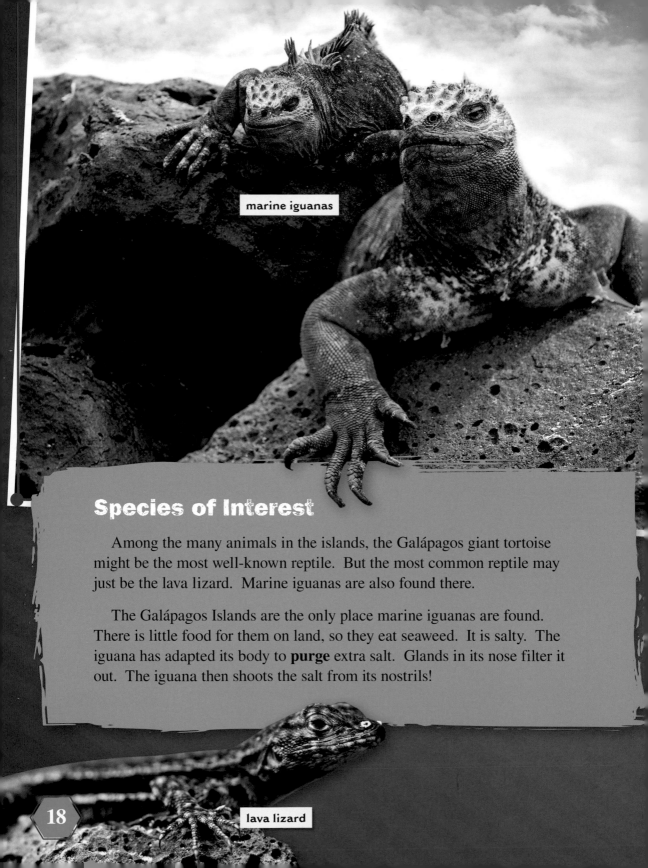

marine iguanas

Species of Interest

Among the many animals in the islands, the Galápagos giant tortoise might be the most well-known reptile. But the most common reptile may just be the lava lizard. Marine iguanas are also found there.

The Galápagos Islands are the only place marine iguanas are found. There is little food for them on land, so they eat seaweed. It is salty. The iguana has adapted its body to **purge** extra salt. Glands in its nose filter it out. The iguana then shoots the salt from its nostrils!

lava lizard

Sally Lightfoot crab

Sally Lightfoots are colorful crabs that are helpful friends of iguanas. They pick ticks off of them.

Other interesting island life includes large painted locusts. They are both colorful and big. In contrast, Galápagos penguins are smaller than you might expect for a penguin. They are also the only penguins north of the equator. Yet, they are in danger. There are fewer than 2,000 of them in the islands.

LET'S EXPLORE MATH

There are fewer than 2,000 Galápagos penguins remaining in the islands. Choose all of the following expressions that show 2,000.

A. $20 \times 10 \times 10 \times 10$

B. 2×10^2

C. 2×10^3

D. 2×10^4

E. $2 \times 10 \times 10 \times 10$

Rodents, such as rats, can be found in abundance in the islands. So can bats of several different species. There are many types of birds as well. One such bird is the flightless cormorant. It's the only bird of its kind that cannot fly. Galápagos finches exist in the islands in at least 13 different species. Darwin studied the finches in detail. He studied how quickly they adapted. Galápagos hawks feast on small animals throughout the islands. Island farmers have long hunted the hawks because they eat their farm animals. Overhunting has put the species in danger.

flightless cormorant

a Darwin's finch

Some of the most unusual looking birds in the islands are the magnificent frigate birds. Males have large red pouches at their throats. They inflate their pouches to attract females. Blue-footed boobies also have a distinct look. They have large blue feet. Males do a special dance with their feet to attract females. The waved albatross mates for life. Partners clack their beaks together and then stop to make a "whoo" sound. People say it seems as though the birds are kissing and cheering.

Galápagos hawk

great frigate bird

blue-footed boobie

seals

From the Sea

Galápagos fur seals are **native** to the islands. They are ocean animals, but they spend more time out of the water than in it. Visitors to the islands often hear the bray of a barking seal **colony**. Galápagos sea lions also live in colonies. They are known to be playful. In fact, they spend a lot of time body surfing!

Dolphins are found in abundance around the islands. Bottlenosed dolphins have short beaks and bulging foreheads. Their sleek bodies move quickly and powerfully through the water. Orcas, or killer whales, actually belong to the dolphin family! They are known for their black bodies and white patches around their eyes. The dorsal fins of adult male orcas can grow very tall. They may **protrude** from the water when orcas swim near the surface. Whales are common around the islands.

Sperm whales, fin whales, blue whales, humpback whales, and more dive through the waters. Some whales can dive very deep. Many can remain below the surface for long periods of time. Visitors to the islands get a thrill when pods of whales **breach**, or break through, the surface.

A humpback whale breaches.

LET'S EXPLORE MATH

Imagine that an orca's dorsal fin extends 1.82 meters from its back.

Choose all of the following expressions that show 1.82.

A. $18.2 \div 10^1$

B. $18.2 \div 10^2$

C. $182 \div 10^1$

D. $182 \div 10^2$

orca

Volunteers rescue a pelican after an oil spill.

Scientists measure the height of a cactus.

Restoring Balance

Protecting the islands is an important focus for **conservationists**. The islands include many at-risk habitats. Some species are threatened. People are working to reverse the damage.

There are some key reasons why animal species become threatened. These include disease, hunting, and loss of habitat. Efforts are being made to combat these threats. Special focus is put on invasive species. They are one of the worst threats to the islands.

Think of invasive animal species like weeds. There is nothing wrong with them. They just do not belong in the **ecosystem**. They use up resources and may kill off some species. They must be removed to restore a natural balance.

Farming and fishing have long been done in the islands. But efforts are made today to do them in more **sustainable** ways. That means they are done in ways that allow people to continue to fish and farm in the future. No land is over-farmed. Fishing is only done to the extent that a species can renew itself. It is important that species keep healthy numbers. In this way, they can continue to exist and help to keep balance in the ecosystem.

A volunteer returns a clean seal to the ocean after an oil spill.

In Human Hands

There was a sentence written outside Lonesome George's enclosure. It read, "Whatever happens to this single animal, let him always remind us that the fate of all living things on Earth is in human hands."

The lesson of the islands is clear. It is one of human responsibility to all living things. Even small things done by people can have big consequences. The sailors who brought three goats to the islands never thought they would one day destroy habitats and species. But they did.

Today, we know so much more than those sailors knew. We know the consequences of what we do. We know that the health of the planet is in our hands. We also know that human efforts can preserve the islands. Efforts are being made today to protect them for tomorrow. We can prevent the loss of more Lonesome Georges and help all species thrive. In that way, island visitors for years to come can enjoy the beauty and wonder that is the Galápagos Islands.

# Problem Solving

Imagine that you are with a team of scientists studying the Galápagos Islands and the wildlife. Your team asks you to do the calculations for the research. Answer the questions to summarize the data.

1. Tortoises move at a very slow rate. They average only about 0.3 kilometers per hour. At this rate, how far will they travel in 10 hours?

2. One scientist tells you that there are only about 1.5×10^4 tortoises left on the island. How many tortoises are there?

3. Some scientists are studying a dolphin pod. If 0.54 of the group are female, what part of the group is male?

4. Other scientists measure 4 lava lizards. All of their lengths are 5.5 centimeters when rounded to the nearest tenth. What could their actual measurements be?

5. Some of the island volcanoes are more than 4,000,000 years old. Write a true equation by writing the missing exponent: $4 \times 10^\square = 4{,}000{,}000$

Glossary

adapts—changes behavior to perform or function better

archipelago—a chain of islands

breach—to make an opening by pushing through something

colony—a group of similar things that live together

conservationists—people who work to protect wildlife and the environment

ecosystem—the combination of all living and nonliving things in an environment

hemisphere—half of a sphere

industries—businesses

native—born in a specific place

poach—to illegally fish or hunt animals

preserved—protected something to keep it in good condition

protrude—to stick out

purge—to force something out

resources—supplies

sustainable—able to be maintained over time without being completely destroyed

tectonic—relating to the rigid plates that make up a planet's crust

tropics—warm weather area of land located near the equator

viable—able to be used

Index

adaptations, 8, 12, 18

blue-footed boobies, 21

conservationists, 25

Darwin, Charles, 8, 20

Ecuador, 6

farming, 4, 25

finch, 8, 20

fishing, 4–5, 25

seal, 22, 25

Galápagos tortoise, 10–16, 18, 28

great blue heron, 17

hunting (poaching), 20, 25

invasive species, 17, 25

lava lizard, 17–18, 28

Lonesome George, 14–15, 26–27

marine iguana, 9, 18

national park, 14, 17

Pinta Island, 14, 16

Sally Lightfoot crab, 9, 19

wild goats, 16

Answer Key

Let's Explore Math

page 5:

The position, or place value, of each digit in a number tells its value. In 108, the digit 8 has a value of 8 ones, or 8. In 89, the digit 8 has a value of 8 tens, or 80.

page 7:

1.

2. $\frac{7}{10}$ or $\frac{70}{100}$; $\frac{5}{100}$

page 11:

1. **a.** 18 m

   b. 180 m

   c. 1,800 m

2. Answers will vary. Example: Each product is 10 times greater than the previous product. This happened because 1.8 was multiplied by a power of 10 that was 10 times greater than the previous power of 10.

page 13:

In 7.7, the first digit has a value of 7 ones, or 7. The second digit has a value of 7 tenths, or $\frac{7}{10}$. The digits are related because 7 ones is 10 times greater than 7 tenths.

page 15:

1.

```
0  0.01 0.02 0.03 0.04 0.05 0.06 0.07 0.08 0.09 0.10
```

2. $\frac{9}{100}$

3. 0.10; The point on the number line shows that $\frac{9}{100}$ is closer to $\frac{10}{100}$ than $\frac{1}{100}$.

page 19:

C, E

page 23:

A, D

Problem Solving

1. 3 km

2. 15,000 tortoises

3. 0.46 male

4. Answers will vary. Examples include 5.47 cm, 5.48 cm, 5.49 cm, 5.51 cm.

5. $4 \times 10^6 = 4{,}000{,}000$